SOUTH CAROLINA

The Palmetto State

BY
JOHN HAMILTON

Abdo & Daughters
An imprint of Abdo Publishing | abdopublishing.com

abdopublishing.com

Published by ABDO Publishing, a division of ABDO, PO Box 398166, Minneapolis, Minnesota 55439. Copyright © 2017 by Abdo Consulting Group, Inc. International copyrights reserved in all countries. No part of this book may be reproduced in any form without written permission from the publisher. ABDO & Daughters™ is a trademark and logo of ABDO Publishing.

Printed in the United States of America, North Mankato, Minnesota.
062016
092016

Editor: Sue Hamilton   **Contributing Editor:** Bridget O'Brien
Graphic Design: Sue Hamilton
Cover Art Direction: Candice Keimig   **Cover Photo Selection:** Neil Klinepier
Cover Photo: iStock
Interior Images: Alamy, AP, Carolina Panthers, Dreamstime, Getty, Granger Collection, iStock, John Hamilton, Library of Congress, Mile High Maps, Mountain High Maps, Minden Pictures, Museum of the Cherokee in South Carolina, NOAA, One Mile Up, Science Source, South Carolina Aquarium, U.S. Dept of Agriculture, U.S. National Park Service, & Wikimedia.

Statistics: *State and City Populations*, U.S. Census Bureau, July 1, 2015 estimates; *Land and Water Area*, U.S. Census Bureau, 2010 Census, MAF/TIGER database; *State Temperature Extremes*, NOAA National Climatic Data Center; *Climatology and Average Annual Precipitation*, NOAA National Climatic Data Center, 1980-2015 statewide averages; *State Highest and Lowest Points*, NOAA National Geodetic Survey.

Websites: To learn more about the United States, visit booklinks.abdopublishing.com. These links are routinely monitored and updated to provide the most current information available.

Cataloging-in-Publication Data

Names: Hamilton, John, 1959- author.
Title: South Carolina / by John Hamilton.
Description: Minneapolis, MN : Abdo Publishing, [2017] | Series: The United
    States of America | Includes index.
Identifiers: LCCN 2015957740 | ISBN 9781680783438 (lib. bdg.) |
    ISBN 9781680774474 (ebook)
Subjects: LCSH: South Carolina--Juvenile literature.
Classification: DDC 975.7--dc23
LC record available at http://lccn.loc.gov/2015957740

CONTENTS

THE PALMETTO STATE

South Carolina is filled with natural beauty. It has long, sandy beaches, blackwater swamps, green forestlands, and towering mountains. It is also known for music festivals, golf courses, and sweetgrass basket weaving. The state's people treasure their traditions and Southern charm. They especially love Southern recipes, from boiled peanuts and deep-fried hush puppies, to shrimp and grits, with hot sauce on everything!

The palmetto is the state tree. A type of palm, they grow by the thousands in the sandy coastal flatlands of South Carolina. Their trunks are soft. They bend in the strong storms that sometimes blow in from the Atlantic Ocean. During the Revolutionary War, soldiers made coastal forts out of the trunks of palmetto trees. British cannonballs did little damage to the sturdy trees. Today, South Carolina is nicknamed "The Palmetto State."

Vacationers enjoy a sunrise walk at Myrtle Beach. The wide, white beaches and warm ocean water make South Carolina's coast a popular tourist destination.

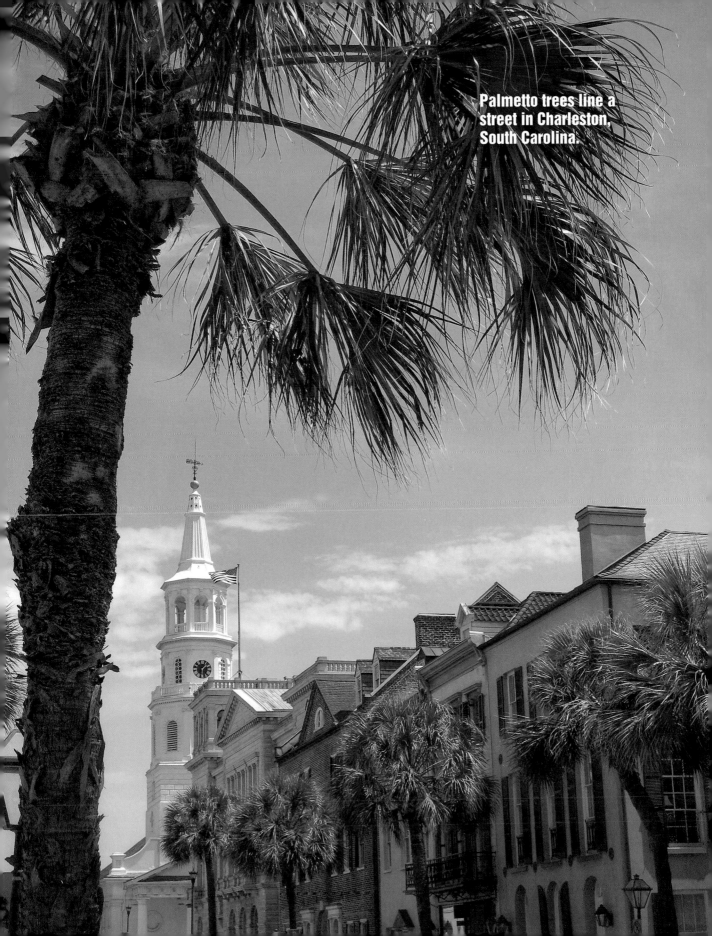

Palmetto trees line a
street in Charleston,
South Carolina.

QUICK FACTS

Name: South Carolina is named after England's King Charles I (1600-1649). The word Carolina is a form of the word *Carolus*, which is a way of writing Charles in Latin.

State Capital: Columbia, population 133,803

Date of Statehood: May 23, 1788 (8th state)

Population: 4,896,146 (23rd-most populous state)

Area (Total Land and Water): 32,020 square miles (82,931 sq km), 40th-largest state

Largest City: Columbia, population 133,803

Nickname: The Palmetto State

Motto: *Dum Spiro Spero* (While I breathe I hope)

State Bird: Carolina Wren

State Flower: Yellow Jessamine

Blue Granite

State Stone: Blue Granite

State Tree: Palmetto

State Songs: "Carolina" and "South Carolina on My Mind"

Palmetto

Highest Point: Sassafras Mountain, 3,560 feet (1,085 m)

Lowest Point: Atlantic Ocean, 0 feet (0 m)

Sassafras Mountain

Average July High Temperature: 91°F (33°C)

Record High Temperature: 113°F (45°C), in Columbia on June 29, 2012

Atlantic Ocean

Average January Low Temperature: 33°F (1°C)

Record Low Temperature: -19°F (-28°C), on Caesars Head on January 21, 1985

Andrew Jackson

Average Annual Precipitation: 47 inches (119 cm)

Number of U.S. Senators: 2

Number of U.S. Representatives: 7

U.S. Presidents Born in South Carolina: Andrew Jackson

U.S. Postal Service Abbreviation: SC

GEOGRAPHY

South Carolina is shaped roughly like an upside-down triangle, with one point facing toward the south. To the southeast is the Atlantic Ocean. The state of North Carolina is to the north. To the southwest, the Savannah River forms the border with the state of Georgia.

In the far northwestern corner of the state are the Blue Ridge Mountains. They are part of the Appalachian Mountains, which stretch from Alabama all the way north to Canada. South Carolina's highest point is in the Blue Ridge Mountains. It is Sassafras Mountain, which soars 3,560 feet (1,085 m) high.

The Jocassee Gorges Wilderness Area is in northwestern South Carolina.

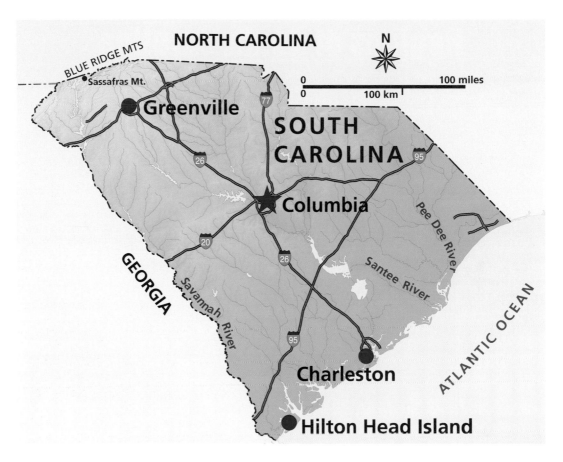

South Carolina's total land and water area is 32,020 square miles (82,931 sq km). It is the 40th-largest state. The state capital is Columbia.

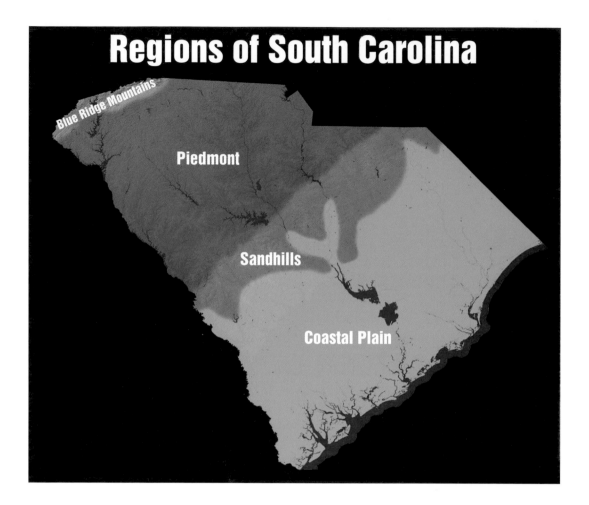

Regions of South Carolina

The Coastal Plain, also called the low country, is in eastern and southeastern South Carolina. It is mainly a flat area that includes marshes and sandy beaches along the Atlantic Ocean. It occupies more than half of the state. Toward the middle of the state, the land rises slightly, with some gently rolling hills.

South Carolina is famous for its coastline, which is 187 miles (301 km) long. In the north, a nearly unbroken stretch of sandy beach extends along the Atlantic Ocean for more than 60 miles (97 km). It is called the Grand Strand. There are many luxury beach resorts in towns such as Myrtle Beach and Surfside Beach.

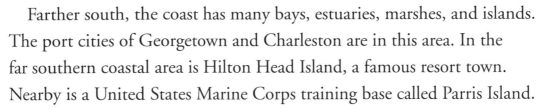
Farther south, the coast has many bays, estuaries, marshes, and islands. The port cities of Georgetown and Charleston are in this area. In the far southern coastal area is Hilton Head Island, a famous resort town. Nearby is a United States Marine Corps training base called Parris Island.

A narrow strip of land just west of the Coastal Plain is called the Sandhills region. It runs diagonally across the state. The ridges in this region are the remains of ancient coastal dunes from when the sea was higher. The capital city of Columbia is in the Sandhills.

Between the Sandhills and the Blue Ridge Mountains is a region called the Piedmont. It occupies almost one-third of the state. There are rolling hills, forests, and farmland.

Major rivers in South Carolina include the Savannah, the Santee, and Pee Dee Rivers. There are no large, natural lakes. However, several reservoirs have been created by constructing hydroelectric dams.

A view of a marine estuary with a palm island on the coast of South Carolina.

GEOGRAPHY

CLIMATE AND WEATHER

South Carolina's summers are hot and humid, thanks to the state's subtropical climate. In winter, the coast is usually mild, while the mountains in the northwest are colder, with some snow.

Statewide, the average July high temperature is 91°F (33°C). The record high is 113°F (45°C), which occurred in Columbia on June 29, 2012.

Coastal South Carolina has hot, humid summers and mild winters.

A satellite view of Hurricane Hugo headed toward South Carolina.

Boats are piled up on shore after Hurricane Hugo struck in 1989.

In January, the average statewide low temperature is 33°F (1°C). The record low temperature occurred on a mountain called Caesars Head on January 21, 1985, in the Blue Ridge Mountains region of the northwest. On that day, the thermometer plunged to -19°F (-28°C).

South Carolina gets plenty of rain. Statewide, the average is 47 inches (119 cm) annually.

Hurricanes sometimes strike South Carolina. They are made powerful by the warm waters of the Atlantic Ocean. Because the state's Coastal Plain is so close to sea level, it is vulnerable to devastating storm surges. A hurricane in 1893 killed up to 2,000 people. In 1989, Hurricane Hugo caused 35 deaths and almost $6 billion in damage in South Carolina.

PLANTS AND
ANIMALS

In the 1600s, South Carolina was almost completely covered in forestland. Today, forests occupy 67 percent of South Carolina's land surface. That equals about 12.9 million acres (5.2 million ha).

The Blue Ridge Mountains are in the northwestern corner of the state. At these high elevations grow hemlock, pine, oak, and hickory trees. In the Piedmont region, in the middle of the state, common trees include oak, hickory, ash, elm, and loblolly pine.

Raven Cliff Falls is in Caesars Head State Park, in northwestern South Carolina.

Spanish moss hangs from live oak trees on a path lined with colorful azaleas.

In the Coastal Plain, there are many oak, hickory, and magnolia trees. There are also longleaf, shortleaf, and loblolly pine. Different kinds of trees grow in the wetlands. They include cypress, tulip, sweet gum, and tupelo trees. Majestic live oaks and bald cypress trees are often draped in sheets of Spanish moss. South Carolina's official state tree is the sable palmetto, commonly called the cabbage palmetto. Often found along the coast, these hardy palm trees usually grow up to 65 feet (20 m) high.

Many kinds of shrubs, trees, and wildflowers give South Carolina's forests and meadows an extra splash of color in the spring. Common wildflowers in the state include lilies, black-eyed Susans, and violets. The official state wildflower is the goldenrod. The state flower is the yellow jessamine.

PLANTS AND ANIMALS

Wild Turkey

White-tailed deer is the official state animal of South Carolina. They can be found in forests statewide. Deer were once hunted nearly to extinction in South Carolina, but careful wildlife management has brought them back in large numbers. Beavers and wild turkeys have made similar comebacks.

Other mammals commonly seen scampering through South Carolina's forests and meadows include striped skunks, river otters, raccoons, muskrats, minks, foxes, coyotes, opossums, southern fox squirrels, and long-tailed weasels. Black bears are the state's largest land mammals. They are found mainly in the Blue Ridge Mountains and the lowland forests near the coast.

Mink

Spotted Salamander

More than 140 species of reptiles and amphibians call South Carolina home. American alligators are found in the Coastal Plain region in swamps and other wetlands. They can grow more than 13 feet (4 m) long and live up to 60 years. The official state amphibian is the spotted salamander. The state reptile is the loggerhead turtle, a threatened species.

There are 38 snake species in South Carolina. That includes six species that are venomous. All snakes help control populations of rodents and other pests.

Hundreds of species of birds make their home in South Carolina. They include bald eagles, bobwhite quails, Canada geese, doves, ducks, pelicans, herons, and egrets. The state bird is the Carolina wren.

Fish found swimming in South Carolina's rivers, lakes, and offshore waters include bluegill, trout, catfish, carp, bass, sunfish, perch, bullheads, red drum, Atlantic croaker, flounder, spadefish, grouper, and snapper.

PLANTS AND ANIMALS

HISTORY

About 12,000 years ago, perhaps even longer, groups of nomadic people first came to the South Carolina area. These Paleo-Indians were the ancient ancestors of today's Native Americans.

Over many centuries, the native people formed separate groups, or tribes. They lived in villages, and learned how to fish and grow crops such as squash and corn. By the time Europeans arrived in the 1500s, several tribes were in the South Carolina area. They included the Cherokee, Catawba, Cusabo, Pee Dee, and Yamasee peoples.

South Carolina's Cherokee people lived in villages, and learned how to fish and grow crops.

Spanish and French explorers sailed to South Carolina in the 1500s and 1600s.

The South Carolina area was first explored by Europeans in 1521, when Francisco Gordillo from Spain arrived. In the years afterwards, both Spain and France tried to start settlements. They failed because of disease, lack of food, and conflicts with Native Americans.

In the 1660s, England created a large colony that includes both today's North and South Carolina. It was called Carolina, in honor of King Charles I. In 1670, Charles Town was built along the banks of the Ashley River. After 10 years, the settlers moved across the river into the area that is now Charleston, South Carolina.

A rice plantation in South Carolina.

The English colony prospered during most of the 1600s and 1700s. Large farms called plantations were built in the lowlands of the Coastal Plain region. There was much money made on goods such as rice, indigo, and furs. Plantation owners forced thousands of African slaves to plant and harvest crops. The bustling city of Charleston became an important trade center of the American colonies.

Between 1710 and 1712, the large colony was unofficially split between north and south. South Carolina officially became a British crown colony in 1729. More settlers poured into the area.

Thousands of Native Americans died because of warfare and from European diseases such as smallpox and measles. Some tried to defend their lands, but they were defeated in battle. Most Native Americans left the area by the 1770s.

In 1776, South Carolina joined the other 12 American colonies in declaring independence from Great Britain. During the Revolutionary War (1775-1783), about 200 battles and skirmishes were fought in South Carolina, more than any other colony. Major battles included Camden, Kings Mountain, and Cowpens. At the Battle of Fort Sullivan, on June 28, 1776, a crude fort made of palmetto logs withstood a furious bombardment by nine British warships. The Patriots returned fire and forced the British ships to retreat, saving the nearby city of Charleston. Today, the palmetto is South Carolina's state tree.

After the war, South Carolina became the 8th state when it ratified, or approved, the United States Constitution on May 23, 1788.

On June 28, 1776, British redcoats tried to invade Charleston, South Carolina, by sea. Blocking the harbor was Sullivan's Island, where the Patriots had a fort of palmetto logs. The spongy logs and sand absorbed the explosions hurled by nine British warships. The Patriots returned fire and forced the British ships to retreat.

After the Revolutionary War, South Carolina continued to grow and prosper. Many large cotton plantations sprang up with the invention of the cotton gin, which made it easy to separate seeds from the cotton fibers. Many landowners became rich. They continued to rely on African slaves to do the hard work of tending to the fields.

During the early 1800s, many South Carolina citizens grew angry over the United States government and its laws. They especially resisted the call to abolish slavery. On December 20, 1860, South Carolina became the first state to secede, or leave, the Union. It joined a group of 11 Southern states called the Confederate States of America. On April 12, 1861, the Civil War (1861-1865) erupted when Confederate troops attacked Fort Sumter, a Union fort in Charleston, South Carolina.

Confederate forces fire on Fort Sumter in Charleston Harbor, South Carolina.

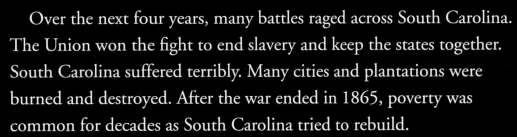
Over the next four years, many battles raged across South Carolina. The Union won the fight to end slavery and keep the states together. South Carolina suffered terribly. Many cities and plantations were burned and destroyed. After the war ended in 1865, poverty was common for decades as South Carolina tried to rebuild.

The state suffered further setbacks. In 1893, a hurricane killed up to 2,000 people and destroyed many homes. In the 1920s, insects called boll weevils destroyed much of the state's cotton crop. And starting in 1929 and lasting through most of the 1930s, the Great Depression caused the state's economy to crash. Thousands of people lost their jobs and businesses.

By the mid-1900s, government spending on large projects such as hydroelectric dams and military bases helped South Carolina's economy. More businesses came to the state. Service industries such as tourism became a major part of the economy. Today, many South Carolina citizens look forward to a much brighter future.

Boll Weevil

23

DID YOU KNOW?

• On April 12, 1861, the first shots of the Civil War were fired by South Carolina Confederate soldiers. They were attacking Union-held Fort Sumter, which rests on a small island in Charleston Harbor. The five-sided fort had walls that were five feet (1.5 m) thick, but after relentless Confederate cannon bombardment, the Union soldiers were forced to surrender the next day. Today, the fort has been preserved as Fort Sumter National Monument. After taking a ferry ride to the island, visitors can walk through the restored fort, tour a museum, and marvel at cannons and many other artifacts from the Civil War.

Fort Sumter

• Sweetgrass basket weaving is a tradition that is more than 300 years old. It originated among African slaves brought to the Charleston and Mount Pleasant areas. They combined West African basket-making techniques with local vegetation to create tightly woven coil baskets with intricate decorative

patterns. Sweetgrass grows in moist, sandy soils near the ocean or wetlands. After drying, the sweetgrass is bundled together and coiled in tight circles. It is held together with thin strands of palmetto fronds. For extra strength and decoration, bulrush and pine needles are added to the design. Sweetgrass basket weaving takes many years to master. Today, skilled craftspeople sell baskets in markets in downtown Charleston and Mount Pleasant.

DID YOU KNOW?

PEOPLE

Andrew Jackson (1767-1845) was the seventh president of the United States. He was born in the Waxhaws border region between North and South Carolina. At just 13 years of age, he joined the military during the Revolutionary War (1775-1783). Orphaned at age 14, he moved to Tennessee, went to school, and became a lawyer. During the War of 1812 (1812-1815), Jackson fought rebellious Native Americans in today's Alabama. In 1815, his troops defended the city of New Orleans, Louisiana, against a much larger force of British redcoats. Jackson's troops said he was as tough as an old stick of hickory wood, which is how he got his nickname, "Old Hickory." He was president of the United States from 1829-1837. Despite being a war hero, Jackson is controversial today because his policies caused the deaths and misery of thousands of Native Americans during the infamous Trail of Tears.

Sarah Grimke and Angelina Grimke Weld fought for rights for all people.

Sarah Grimke (1792-1873) and her sister, **Angelina Grimke Weld** (1805-1879), were born in Charleston, South Carolina. They were daughters of a rich farmer and slave owner. After witnessing the abuse of African Americans, they grew to hate slavery. As adults, they became abolitionists who wanted the practice of slavery abolished. They joined anti-slavery groups and gave lectures all over the country. They also wrote many articles urging people to give up slavery. They later became involved in the women's suffrage movement. They spoke out against the poor treatment of women, and fought for equal rights.

PEOPLE

Francis Marion (1732-1795) was born in Berkeley County, South Carolina. He was a plantation owner who became a military officer during the French and Indian War (1754-1763). During the Revolutionary War (1775-1783), he used his knowledge of the South Carolina backcountry wilderness to fight British soldiers. He and his troops used the element of surprise to attack the redcoats and then seemingly disappear into the forests. The frustrated British nicknamed him "The Swamp Fox."

Dizzy Gillespie (1917-1993) was one of the greatest jazz trumpeters who ever lived. He was also a bandleader and composer. Born in Cheraw, South Carolina, his real name was John Birks Gillespie. He went by the name "Dizzy" because he liked to goof around. He taught himself how to play trombone and trumpet by the time he was 12. He was a wizard at improvising jazz music, and was easily recognizable for his bent horn and puffed-out cheeks. He was a founder of a jazz style called bebop.

Joe Frazier (1944-2011) was one of the greatest boxers to ever enter the ring. Known for his punching power, he became a gold medal winner at the 1964 Summer Olympic Games in Tokyo, Japan. As a professional, Frazier became the world heavyweight champion from 1970-1973. He had a powerful left hook that he used to knock out his opponents. Nicknamed "Smokin' Joe," his most famous victory came in 1971 when he defeated his rival, Muhammad Ali. (Ali would later beat Frazier in 1974, and retake the heavyweight crown in 1975). Frazier finished his professional career with a record of 32 wins, 4 losses, and 1 tie. He was inducted into the International Boxing Hall of Fame and the World Boxing Hall of Fame. After retirement, he opened a gym to train young boxers. Frazier was born and raised in Beaufort, South Carolina.

CITIES

Columbia is the largest city in South Carolina. It is also the state capital. Its population is about 133,803. In 1786, state lawmakers decided to create a town in central South Carolina to serve as the new state capital. Today, Columbia is a center for business. Major employers include government, health care, education, insurance, and transportation. The University of South Carolina is in the city. It is the largest university in the state, enrolling more than 33,000 students each year. Fort Jackson is a United States Army base that trains more than 35,000 new soldiers annually. Columbia's South Carolina State Museum is the largest museum in the state. It has many exhibits that highlight the art, science, and cultural history of South Carolina.

Charleston is a major port along South Carolina's Atlantic Ocean coast. First settled by English colonists in 1670, it was named Charles Town in honor of King Charles II. In 1783, it became known as Charleston. Today, its population is approximately 132,609, which makes it the state's second-largest city. Together with its suburbs, it is home to more than 725,000 people. In addition to being a busy shipping port, Charleston has many historic sites. It is a popular tourist destination. Fort Sumter, the place where the first shots of the Civil War were fired in 1861, rests on an island in Charleston Harbor. The College of Charleston was founded in 1770, and enrolls more than 11,000 students yearly.

CITIES

Greenville is in northwestern South Carolina. Its population is about 64,579. It is part of a rapidly growing area of the state. Nearby is another city, called Spartanburg. Together with Spartanburg and other nearby towns, the area is home to more than 1.5 million people. Greenville was founded in 1831. It became a mill city in the late 1800s. Textile factories used the Reedy River to power their machinery. Today, Greenville continues to attract manufacturers and other businesses that make products such as textiles, automotive parts, chemicals, paper, and electronics. For a city of its size, Greenville has many concert halls, dance troupes, and art galleries. The Greenville County Museum of Art displays masterpieces of American artwork, including many watercolors by the famous painter Andrew Wyeth.

SOUTH CAROLINA

Harbour Town Lighthouse on Hilton Head Island.

An alligator eating a blue crab.

Great Blue Heron

Hilton Head Island is the name of a town located in the southeastern part of the state along the Atlantic Ocean coast. It is also the name of the island upon which the town rests. Often simply called Hilton Head, the town was named for William Hilton. He was an English sea captain who explored the island in 1663. Early settlers of the 1800s grew rice, cotton, and sugar cane. Today, Hilton Head Island is a resort community, with a population of about 40,512. Cotton fields have been replaced by world-class golf courses and tennis courts. There continues to be much natural beauty to explore along the coast. Bottlenose dolphins, loggerhead turtles, manatees, alligators, and hundreds of bird species are commonly spotted.

TRANSPORTATION

There are 66,232 miles (106,590 km) of public roadways in South Carolina. Several interstate highways crisscross the state. Interstates I-85, I-20, and I-95 angle southwest-to-northeast across the state. Interstate I-26 angles southeast-to-northwest, connecting Charleston, Columbia, and Greenville. Interstate I-77 travels north out of Columbia and connects with Charlotte, North Carolina, just across the state line.

There are 15 freight railroads operating in South Carolina on 2,311 miles (3,719 km) of track. The most common bulky goods hauled by rail in the state include coal, chemicals, lumber, paper, and metal products. Amtrak operates four routes that whisk passengers across the state, including the Crescent, Palmetto, Silver Meteor, and Silver Star lines.

A CSX freight train rumbles through Allendale, South Carolina.

A container ship is unloaded at the Port of Charleston.

The Port of Charleston ranks in the top 10 among the busiest ports in the United States. The deepwater harbor services more than 1,900 vessels yearly. Dockworkers load and unload approximately 1 million containers plus 1.4 million tons (1.3 million metric tons) of non-container cargo each year.

South Carolina's busiest commercial airport is Charleston International Airport. It services more than 3.4 million passengers yearly.

TRANSPORTATION

NATURAL
RESOURCES

There are about 24,400 farms operating in South Carolina. Most are small, with an average size of 205 acres (83 ha). In total, farms occupy about 5 million acres of land, which is 26 percent of South Carolina's land area.

In the 1800s, cotton was South Carolina's most important crop. Today, cotton is grown in just a few places in the Coastal Plain region. The most valuable crops grown in South Carolina today include soybeans, hay, corn for livestock, peanuts, tobacco, melons, and cotton.

A bale of cotton on a South Carolina farm. Cotton is grown in just a few places in the Coastal Plain region.

Crates of peaches are ready to go to a packing shed at an orchard in Kline, South Carolina.

Many South Carolina farmers make a living selling greenhouse and nursery plants and flowers. Like neighboring Georgia, South Carolina is famous for its juicy peaches. The most valuable livestock products include broiler chickens, hogs, and dairy cows.

The most valuable products mined in South Carolina include crushed stone for construction, granite, kaolin (a type of clay), plus sand and gravel.

Commercial fishing is not as big as it once was in South Carolina because of foreign competition and overfishing. The most valuable catches today include shrimp, oysters, crabs, and clams.

South Carolina has about 12.9 million acres (5.2 million ha) of forestland. That is 67 percent of the state's total land area. The forest industry employs more than 90,000 people in South Carolina.

NATURAL RESOURCES

INDUSTRY

For much of the 20th century, manufacturing was the most important part of South Carolina's economy. Factories and mills turned the state's cotton crop into clothing and many other products. Today, textiles aren't as important to South Carolina's economy. However, the state's factories continue to make many other kinds of products, including paper, machinery, chemicals, and plastics. Many companies make automobiles and vehicle parts in South Carolina, including BMW, Honda, and Freightliner.

Automobiles move down the assembly line at the BMW Manufacturing Company in Greer, South Carolina.

South Carolina's white, sandy beaches bring millions of tourists to the area.

As in many other states, the service industry has become more important to South Carolina in recent years. Instead of manufacturing products, service industries sell services to businesses and consumers. It includes businesses such as advertising, financial services, health care, insurance, restaurants, retail stores, law, marketing, and tourism. Today, about 57 percent of South Carolinians are employed in the service industry.

Tourism has become a big part of South Carolina's economy in recent years. Millions of people are drawn to the state's many historic sites, sandy beaches, and luxury resorts. Tourism adds more than $19 billion to the state's economy yearly, and provides for almost 200,000 jobs.

SPORTS

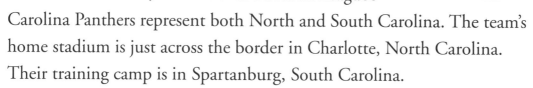

South Carolina has no professional major league sports teams of its own. However, the National Football League's Carolina Panthers represent both North and South Carolina. The team's home stadium is just across the border in Charlotte, North Carolina. Their training camp is in Spartanburg, South Carolina.

South Carolina has several professional minor league teams that compete in the state. They play baseball, ice hockey, soccer, and basketball.

College sports are very popular in South Carolina, especially football. The two most popular teams—the Clemson University Tigers and the University of South Carolina Gamecocks—draw tens of thousands of fans to each home game.

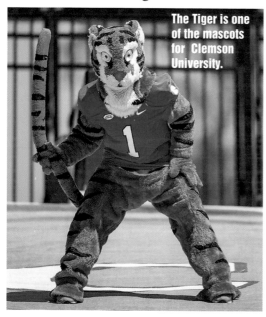

The Tiger is one of the mascots for Clemson University.

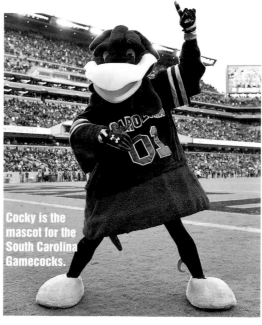

Cocky is the mascot for the South Carolina Gamecocks.

The egg-shaped, 1.37-mile (2.2-km) Darlington Raceway opened in 1950 and became known as "The Track Too Tough to Tame."

As in most Southern states, NASCAR racing is huge in South Carolina. Darlington Raceway is nicknamed "The Track Too Tough to Tame." It hosts several NASCAR stock car races, including the popular Southern 500 over Labor Day.

For outdoor lovers, there is much to do in South Carolina. Hikers enjoy traveling through the forested Blue Ridge Mountains, which are home to many beautiful waterfalls. The Atlantic Ocean coast is a favorite destination for swimming, fishing, and boating. South Carolina is also famous for its many golf courses.

ENTERTAINMENT

South Carolina is filled with historic sites. Many have been preserved as national parks, and honor events from the Revolutionary War and the Civil War. Cowpens National Battlefield and Kings Mountain National Military Park are Revolutionary War sites near Gaffney, South Carolina, in the northwestern part of the state. Fort Sumter National Monument is a very popular park in Charleston. It marks the spot where the first shots of the Civil War were fired.

Reenactors give a demonstration of Revolutionary War weapons at Cowpens National Battlefield.

South Carolina Aquarium

Sea Turtle

Sand Tiger Shark

Charleston was an important center of the arts in the 1700s. The first opera in America was performed in the city. Today, Charleston continues to feature the performing arts through theater, dance, and music. For architecture lovers, there are many buildings from the 1700s that are preserved in the city.

The South Carolina Aquarium in Charleston is located along the historic Charleston Harbor waterfront. It is home to more than 5,000 animals, including sharks, jellyfish, alligators, river otters, and loggerhead turtles.

Spoleto Festival USA is an annual performing arts festival held throughout Charleston. The celebration showcases dance, theater, opera, choir, jazz, and classical music.

ENTERTAINMENT

TIMELINE

10,000 BC—Paleo-Indians arrived in the land called South Carolina today. They were nomads who hunted large herds of animals.

1500s—Native American tribes living in the South Carolina area included the Catawba, Cusabo, Pee Dee, Cherokee, and Yamasee peoples.

1521—Spaniard Francisco Gordillo leads an expedition that sails along the South Carolina coast.

1670—The English begin a settlement near present-day Charleston.

1729—South Carolina officially becomes a British colony.

1775-1783—The Revolutionary War is fought. About 200 battles and skirmishes rage throughout South Carolina, more than any other colony.

1788—South Carolina ratifies the United States Constitution and becomes the 8th state in the Union.

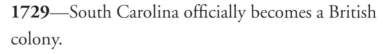

1861—The first shots of the Civil War are fired at Fort Sumter in Charleston.

Charleston in ruins.

1861-1865—South Carolina suffers much destruction during the Civil War.

1920s—Boll weevils destroy much of the state's cotton crop.

1929—The Great Depression begins. South Carolina's economy suffers.

1960s-1970s—The state's economy expands. Manufacturing and tourism become much more important.

1989—Hurricane Hugo hits South Carolina, causing 35 deaths and $6 billion in damage in South Carolina.

2003—South Carolina's Senator Strom Thurmond retires at age 100, after 48 years of service in the United States Senate.

2015—The divisive Confederate flag is taken down from the South Carolina State House in Columbia.

GLOSSARY

BEBOP

A kind of jazz music that was invented in the United States in the 1940s. It has a very fast tempo, with complex chords, key changes, and many improvised solos.

CIVIL WAR

The war fought between America's Northern and Southern states from 1861-1865. The Southern states were for slavery. They wanted to start their own country. Northern states fought against slavery and a division of the country.

CONFEDERACY

The Southern states of Alabama, Arkansas, Florida, Georgia, Louisiana, Mississippi, North Carolina, South Carolina, Tennessee, Texas, and Virginia. These states wanted to keep slavery legal. They broke away from the United States during the Civil War and formed their own country, known as the Confederate States of America, or simply the Confederacy. The Confederacy dissolved in 1865 when the war ended.

INDIGO

A tropical plant that is used to make a dark blue dye, which is often used to color cloth.

MARSH

A wetland that has many grasses and reeds. They are often found at the edges of lakes and streams.

NASCAR

National Association for Stock Car Auto Racing. A popular sporting event with races held across the United States. The Darlington Raceway, near the city of Darlington, South Carolina, hosts many NASCAR races.

NOMADS

People who don't live in one place. Nomads are constantly traveling, usually following animal herds, which they hunt for food.

PIEDMONT

An Italian word that means "at the foot of the mountains."

SECEDE

To withdraw from a membership or alliance. Just before the Civil War began, the states of the Southern Confederacy seceded from the United States.

STORM SURGE

When hurricane winds push the ocean's water onto land. The rise in the water level can flood low-lying areas, such as islands, cities, and farms. Storm surges can be deadly.

SWAMP

A wetland that has many trees and large shrubs.

TRAIL OF TEARS

In the last years of the 1700s, land-hungry settlers began migrating westward. In 1838 and 1839, thousands of Cherokee, Creek, and other Native Americans were forced to move west to Oklahoma. Today, the brutal trek is called the Trail of Tears. The Native American land was turned over to plantation owners, who grew cotton and other cash crops. The plantations required many slaves to harvest the crops cheaply.

INDEX